New Wheels

by Catherine Baker

illustrated by Esther Hernando

Tomas enjoyed playing in the park with Beth. They would giggle at the same jokes.

They always found plenty of things to do.

One day, Beth had a new bike. She rode it to the park.

The bike was blue with lights on the wheels.
A silver bell sparkled on the handlebars.

Tomas looked longingly at the bike.

"Can I have a go, please?" Tomas asked.

"Not today," said Beth.

"I had to wait for this bike," said Beth.
"What if you dented it?"

Then she rode away.

Tomas walked back to his mum slowly.

“Are you all right, Tomas?” asked Mum.

“Beth has a new bike,” said Tomas.
“She didn’t let me ride it.”

“I would love a new bike,” said Tomas.
“Then I could ride to the park with Beth.”

"You will get a bike one day," said Mum.
"Sometimes, we have to wait for things."

Mum jumped up!

"Let's make something you can ride now," she said. "Come on!"

At home, Mum went into the shed. She found a saw and some junk.

“What are these boxes for?” asked Tomas.

"We are going to make a go-kart!" said Mum.

"Wow!" exclaimed Tomas.

Mum hammered some wheels on to a box.
Tomas helped.

Beth came to the gate.

“I’m sorry I didn’t let you ride my bike. I wanted to ride it first,” said Beth.

"It's fine," said Tomas, giving Beth a smile.

"What are you doing?" asked Beth.

"I am finishing my go-kart," said Tomas.

“Wow,” said Beth. “You are lucky! I have never made anything like that.”

"You can help if you want to," said Tomas.

Once the go-kart was finished, they painted it blue. Tomas beamed.

Mum added its name: *Whizzing Wheels*.
Then they went to the park for a race.

Beth was going to ride her bike. Tomas was going to ride in his new go-kart!

Who came first in the race? It was a tie!

Look Back

Encourage students to use the pictures to retell the story.